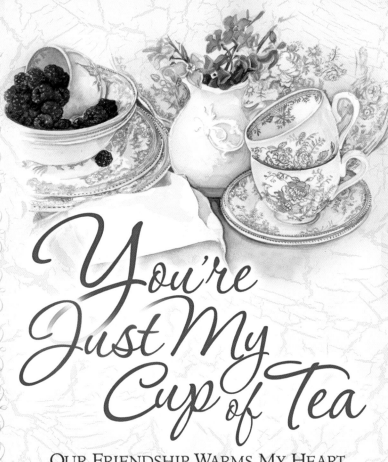

You're Just My Cup of Tea

Our Friendship Warms My Heart

Paintings by

CAMILLE ELLERBROOK

HARVEST HOUSE PUBLISHERS

EUGENE, OREGON

You're Just My Cup of Tea

Copyright © 2006 by Harvest House Publishers
Eugene, Oregon 97402

ISBN-13: 978-0-7369-1793-3
ISBN-10: 0-7369-1793-4

The artwork of Camille Ellerbrook © 2006 is used by Harvest House Publishers, Inc. under authorization from Indigo Gate, Inc. For more information regarding art prints featured in this book, please contact:

> Gifford B. Bowne II
> Indigo Gate, Inc.
> 1 Pegasus Drive
> Colts Neck, NJ 07722

Design and production by Garborg Design Works, Inc., Minneapolis, Minnesota
Harvest House Publishers has made every effort to trace the ownership of all poems and quotes. In the event of a question arising from the use of a poem or quote, we regret any error made and will be pleased to make the necessary correction in future editions of this book.

Printed in China
07 08 09 10 11 12 13 /LP/ 10 9 8 7 6 5 4 3 2

Miss Sanxay drank tea with us—a very happy day in my brother and sister's company. She is one of the most charming women I know—amiable in her person, lively in discourse, of the sweetest temper and most benevolent disposition—in music an angel, and clever at every thing. We work, we chat, we walk and are happy together.

From the journal of Agnes Porter

Come along inside...We'll see if tea and buns can make the world a better place.

Kenneth Grahame

The Wind in the Willows

It is around the table that friends understand best the warmth of being together.

Italian Proverb

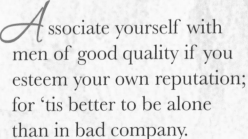

*A*ssociate yourself with men of good quality if you esteem your own reputation; for 'tis better to be alone than in bad company.

George Washington

When friends ask for a second cup
they are open to conversation.

Gail Parent

SPICED HONEY STARS

These delicious little cookies are daintily spiced with a hint of orange.
This recipe makes about 5 dozen cookies.

> ½ cup butter, softened
> ¾ cup sugar
> 1 egg
> ¼ cup honey
> grated peel of one small orange
> 2 cups flour
> 1 teaspoon baking soda
> 1 teaspoon cinnamon
> ½ teaspoon ground ginger
> ¼ teaspoon ground cloves

Royal Icing (recipe on page 14) and silver baking ornaments

Preheat oven to 375°. Cream butter and sugar together thoroughly, then
add eggs, honey, and orange peel and beat until smooth. Sift together
flour, soda, and spices, then stir into butter mixture. Turn dough out onto
well-floured surface (dough will be soft) and roll to ⅛-inch thickness. Cut
out cookies with a 2-inch star-shaped cutter. Bake on ungreased cookie
sheet for 7-8 minutes. Let stand for a few minutes before removing to wire
racks to cool. Decorate as desired with *Royal Icing* and little silver candies.

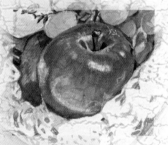

*S*urely every one is aware of the divine pleasures
which attend a wintry fireside; candles at four o'clock,
warm hearth rugs, tea, a fair tea-maker, shutters
closed, curtains flowing in ample draperies to the floor,
while the wind and rain are raging audibly without.

Thomas De Quincey

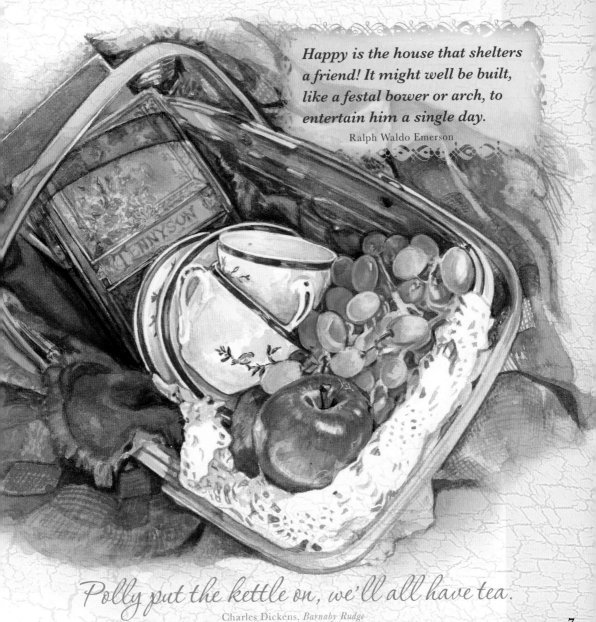

*Happy is the house that shelters
a friend! It might well be built,
like a festal bower or arch, to
entertain him a single day.*

Ralph Waldo Emerson

Polly put the kettle on, we'll all have tea.

Charles Dickens, *Barnaby Rudge*

7

The mind never unbends itself so agreeably as in the conversation of a well-chosen friend. There is indeed no blessing of life that is any way comparable to the enjoyment of a discreet and virtuous friend. It eases and unloads the mind, clears and improves the understanding, engenders thought and knowledge, animates virtue and good resolutions, soothes and allays the passions, and finds employment for most of the vacant hours of life.

Joseph Addison

It is the best and truest friend who honestly tells us the truth about ourselves even when he knows we shall not like it.

R.C.H. Lenski

The very best thing is good talk, and the thing that helps it most is friendship.

Henry Van Dyke

IRISH OATMEAL SCONES

Scones don't have to look like biscuits or wedges. This easy variation came from a farmhouse in Ireland. Enjoy with sweet jam and imitation clotted cream. This recipe will make 12 muffin-shaped scones.

Nonstick cooking spray
¾ cup milk or cream
1 large egg
3-4 tablespoons light brown sugar
1 teaspoon vanilla
2 ¼ cups all-purpose flour
1 cup old-fashioned rolled oats
1 tablespoon double-acting baking powder
½ teaspoon baking soda
½ teaspoon salt
¾ stick (6 tablespoons) cold, unsalted butter, cut into small pieces
½ cup dried currants (or raisins)

Spray a 12-cup muffin pan with nonstick spray and set aside. In a bowl, whisk together milk, egg, brown sugar, and vanilla. In another bowl, stir together dry ingredients. Use a pastry blender or two knives to cut butter into dry ingredients until mixture resembles coarse meal. Stir in the currants and the milk mixture until mixture just forms a sticky dough. Drop by ⅓-cup measures into prepared muffin cups and bake in the middle of a preheated 400° oven for 15-18 minutes, or until golden.

Join Me for Tea by Emilie Barnes

Somehow, taking tea together encourages an atmosphere of intimacy when you sleep off the timepiece in your mind and cast your fate to a delight of tasty tea, tiny foods, and thoughtful conversation.

Gail Greco

Read this my dears, and you will see
how to make a nice cup of tea
take teapot to kettle, not t'other way round
and when you hear that whistling sound
pour a little in the pot
just to make it nice and hot.
Pour that out and put in the tea,
loose or in bags, your choice, you see.
One bag for each two cups will do
with one extra bag to make a fine brew.
Steep 3-5 minutes then pour a cup.
Then sit right down and drink it up!

Patricia Winchester
Afternoon Teas

Friends are needed both for joy and for sorrow.
Samuel Paterson

Let's be merry; we'll have
tea and toast…and an
endless host of syllabubs
and jellies and mince-pies.

Percy Bysshe Shelley

Those who bring sunshine
to the lives of others cannot
keep it from themselves.

Sir James Barrie

No one is useless in the world
who lightens the burden of it
for anyone else.

Charles Dickens

he language of friendship is not words but meanings.

Henry David Thoreau

*Perhaps the most delightful friend-
ships are those in which there is
much agreement, much disputation,
and yet more personal liking.*

George Eliot

*There are high spots in all of our lives
and most of them have come about through
encouragement from someone else.*

George M. Adams

recipe

ROYAL ICING

2 teaspoons powdered egg whites (meringue powder)
2⅔ cups confectioners' sugar
¼ cup water

Combine all ingredients and beat with electric mixer for
8-10 minutes, until peaks form and icing is the texture of
sour cream. Thin icing with water a drop at a time until
about consistency of honey. For each cookie, place a dollop
of icing in the center and use a knife tip or chopstick to
spread the thin icing on top of the cookie, leaving edges
brown. Let icing harden before serving or storing cookies.

Join Me for Tea by Emilie Barnes

recipe

On the pa

A friend is someone we turn to
when our spirits need a lift,
A friend is someone we treasure,
for our friendship is a gift.
A friend is someone who fills our
lives with beauty, joy, and grace
And makes the world we live in a
better and happier place.

Author Unknown

...ween the homes of friends, the grass does not grow.

Norwegian Proverb

YOU ARE BLESSED WITH GOOD FRIENDS

[Mrs. Jesse] poured tea. The oil-lamps cast a warm light on the teatray. The teapot was china, with little roses painted all over it, crimson and blush-pink and celestial blue, and the cups were garlanded with the same flowers. There were sugared biscuits, each with a flower made out of piped icing, creamy, violet, snow-white. Sophy Sheekhy watched the stream of topaz-coloured liquid fall from the spout, steaming and aromatic. This too was a miracle, that gold-skinned persons in China and bronze-skinned persons in India should gather leaves which should come across the seas safely in white-winged ships, encased in lead, encased in wood, surviving storms and whirlwinds, sailing on under hot sun and cold moon, and come here, and be poured from bone china, made from fine clay, moulded by clever fingers, in the Pottery Towns, baked in kilns, glazed with slippery shiny clay, baked again, painted with rosebuds by artist-hands holding fine, fine brushes, delicately turning the potter's wheel and implanting, with a kiss of sable-hairs, floating buds on an azure ground, or a dead white ground, and that sugar should be fetched where black men and women slaved and died terribly to make these delicate flowers that melted on the tongue like the scrolls in the mouth of the Prophet Isaiah, that flour should be milled, and milk shaken into butter, and both worked together into these momentary delights, baked in Mrs. Jesse's oven and piled elegantly onto a plate to be offered to Captain Jesse with his wool-white head and smiling eyes, to Mrs. Papagay, flushed and agitated, to her sick self, and the black bird and the dribbling Pug, in front of the hot coals of fire, in the benign lamplight. Any of them might so easily have not been there to drink the tea, or eat the sweetmeats. Storms and ice-floes might have taken Captain Jesse, grief or childbearing might have destroyed his wife, Mrs. Papagay might have lapsed into penury, and she herself have died as an overworked servant, but here they were and their eyes were bright and their tongues tasted goodness.

A.S. Byatt

The Conjugal Angel

e sip of this will bathe the drooping spirits
elight, beyond the bliss of dreams.

Milton

YOU ARE BLESSED WITH GOOD FRIENDS

ROSEMARY CHEDDAR MUFFINS

A savory and delicious twist on a traditional muffin. If you like these, try substituting other herbs such as basil, thyme, or a fines herbes mixture for the rosemary.

2 cups unsifted all-purpose flour
2 tablespoons baking powder
½ teaspoon salt
2 eggs
1 tablespoon honey

1 cup milk
2 tablespoons fresh rosemary, chopped
⅛ teaspoon cayenne or dried mustard
½ cup sharp cheddar, finely shredded

Heat oven to 400°. Grease regular-sized muffin tin with oil or cooking spray or line with paper liners. Sift the dry ingredients together and stir in the cheese and rosemary. In another bowl, beat the eggs, then add the oil, honey, and milk. Combine the dry and liquid ingredients and mix just until blended. Pour batter into muffin cups, sprinkle with a little extra cheese, and bake for 25 minutes or until done. Let cool slightly before removing from pan.

Join Me for Tea by Emilie Barnes

recipe

*There are few hours
in life more agreeable
than the hour dedicated
to the ceremony known
as afternoon tea.*

Henry James, *Portrait of a Lady*

Tea is drunk to
forget the din of
the world.

T'ien Yiheng

No man is useless while he has a friend.

Robert Louis Stevenson

19

Chaim Potok, *The Chosen*

Christopher Robin
was home by this
time, because it was
the afternoon, and
he was so glad to see
them that they stayed
there until very nearly
tea-time, and then
they had a Very Near-
ly tea, which is one
you forget about after-
wards, and hurried on
to Pooh Corner, so as
to see Eeyore before it
was too late to have a
Proper Tea with Owl.

A.A. Milne
The House at Pooh Corner

**But friendship is precious, not
only in the shade, but in the
sunshine of life; and thanks to
a benevolent arrangement of
things, the greater part of life
is sunshine.**

Thomas Jefferson

I have always felt that
the great high privilege of
friendship was that one
had to explain nothing.

Katherine Mansfield

If you want an accounting of your worth, count your friends.

Merry Browne

Of all the means which wisdom uses to ensure happiness throughout the whole of life, by far the most important is the acquisition of friends.

Epicurus

Where there's tea there's hope—

Sir Arthur Pinero

"NOT REALLY FROM DEVONSHIRE" CREAM

It's almost impossible to find real English clotted cream here in the United States. This delicious dairy mixture makes an acceptable substitute. Real comfort food!

½ pint whipping cream
1 tablespoon sour cream
3 tablespoons confectioners' sugar

Chill bowl and beaters, then whip all ingredients together. Keep refrigerated. Serve with scones.

Join Me for Tea by Emilie Barnes

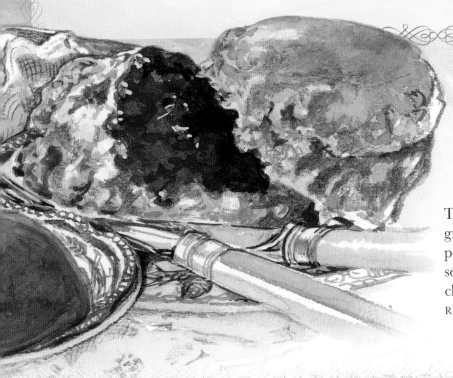

There is a great deal of poetry and fine sentiment in a chest of tea.

Ralph Waldo Emerson

The cozy fire is bright and gay,
The merry kettle boils away
And hums a cheerful song.
I sing the saucer and the cup;
Pray, Mary, fill the teapot up,
And do not make it strong.

Barry Pain

The Poets at Tea, Cowper

What greater thing is there for two human souls than to feel that they are joined together to strengthen each other in all labour, to minister to each other in all sorrow, to share with each other in all gladness, to be one with each other in the silent unspoken memories?

George Eliot

To: My dear Friend
Happy Holidays
From: Catherine

*We cannot tell the precise moment when
friendship is formed. As in filling a vessel drop
by drop, there is at last a drop which makes it
run over; so in a series of kindnesses there is at
last one which makes the heart run over.*

Samuel Johnson

25

*Y*es we are
[friends] and
I do like to pass
the day with
you in serious
and inconse-
quential chat-
ter. I wouldn't
mind washing
up beside you,
dusting beside
you, reading the
back half of the
paper while you
read the front.
We are friends
and I would
miss you, do
miss you and
think of you
very often.

Jeanette Winterson

The greatest good
you can do for
another is not just
to share your riches
but to reveal to him
his own.

Benjamin Disraeli

ong years you've kept the door ajar
o greet me, coming from afar.
ong years in my accustomed place
ve read my welcome in your face.

Robert Bridges

Friends do not live in harmony merely, as some say, but in melody.

Henry David Thoreau

A CELEBRATION TABLE

If you own a glass-topped dining table, you can add a refreshing twist to your celebration table with just a little paint. Simply clean the underside of your table with commercial glass cleaner and use acrylic craft paints to dot colorful confetti directly on the glass.

If you like, you could even get very creative and paint festive garlands around the table's edge or words of congratulations to the guest of honor—just remember to paint backward so the words will read correctly from the top. This technique adapts very easily to any kind of glass—from the inside of the storm door to the coffee tables in the living room or even your glass plates. (Just be sure to paint on the undersides so that the paint doesn't interfere with the food.) When you're through with the party, you'll find the paint comes off easily with a spritz of glass cleaner and some paper towels.

Join Me for Tea by Emilie Barnes

recipe

He who sows courtesy reaps friendship, and he who plants kindness gathers love.

Saint Basil

We attract hearts by the qualities we display; we retain them by the qualities we possess.

Jean Baptiste Antoine Suard

The feeling of friendship is like that of being comfortably filled with roast beef.

Samuel Johnson

Now stir the fire, and close the shutters fast,
Let fall the curtains, wheel the sofa round,
And, while the bubbling and loud hissing urn
Throws up a steamy column and the cups
That cheer but not inebriate, wait on each,
So let us welcome peaceful ev'ning in.

William Cowper

CELEBRATION SANDWICHES

These colorful sandwiches will really tingle your
taste buds and delight your eye.

> 2 6-ounce cans water-packed tuna, drained
> 2 tablespoons mayonnaise
> 4 teaspoons finely diced green bell pepper
> 4 teaspoons finely diced red bell pepper
> 2 tablespoons red onion, finely diced
> ½ teaspoon chopped, fresh parsley
> 1 teaspoon rice wine vinegar
> ½ teaspoon lemon juice
> 7 drops hot pepper sauce
> salt and white pepper to taste
> 1 loaf fine-textured white or wheat bread
> unsalted butter, softened

Combine all ingredients but bread and butter and
mix well. Refrigerate at least one hour. Spread
each slice of bread with softened butter. Spread
half the slices with tuna mixture, then top with
remaining slices. With a serrated knife, cut off
crusts and cut sandwiches into three or four
fingers. Wrap tightly in plastic wrap or cover with
a damp tea towel until ready to serve.

Join Me for Tea by Emilie Barnes

We need old friends to help us gr

Letty Collin Pogrebin

Sept. 2007

My dear Angelica,

I'm not good with words, and even less expressive
with feelings. However, you know me well
enough to understand I'm a faithful and
devoted friend.

We've covered many years traveling on different
paths, with dissimilar interests and certainly
unlike lifestyles. (You came from Brooklyn!)

Nonetheless, we have been brought together, now
traveling the most beautiful road, with one true
interest and love by and through HIM.

Oh how blessed am I to have this great gift.
You, Angelica, and your wonderful family.

more healthy and prosperous years –
remaining "just as you are" – "just
my cup of tea."

Much love and prayers
Vera

I found this little book + to be just the right
one to express how I feel. It's delicate, warm
and personal, without being "mushy," and says
what I cannot!

So on this, your day, I thank God for you,
my blessing, and hope you enjoy many

Friendship: Gentle as
the dew from the silken
skies; radiant as some
glorious diadem, set
with countless stars.

Yeoman Shield

and new friends to help us stay young.

Enjoy life sip by sip not gulp by gulp.

The Minister of Leaves